Coloring Your World

"The Essentials"

An Introduction To Adult Coloring

By Ian Kirk

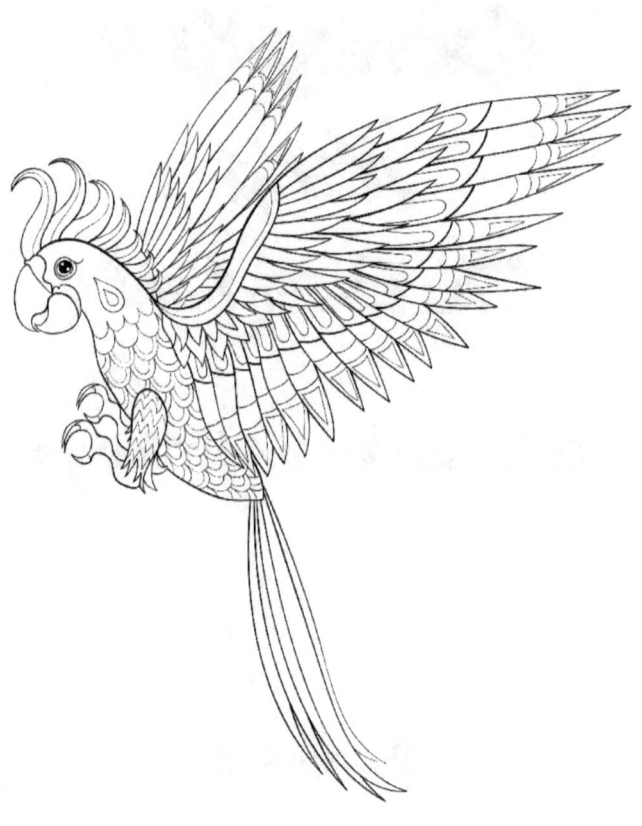

Dedication

To my Lord who saved my life

To my beloved wife whom I will love always

To my five children who are leaders of the

next generation

To my dear friend Joe who is one of the wisest and

compassionate people I know

Coloring Your World
"The Essentials"

Coloring has therapeutic potential to reduce anxiety, create focus or bring about more mindfulness. Like meditation, coloring allows the brain to switch off other thoughts and focus.

- CNN Health, Jan 6, 2016

Coloring, and art in general, is a good, healthy way to reduce stress, said Sarah Bashus, a social worker and therapist at Sanford -

Bismarck Tribune, Feb 15, 2016

Lacy Mucklow says she sees the coloring craze as a healthy way for stressed-out multitaskers to tune out the larger world. "It's good for us to be quiet and still and focused on just one thing for once."

- USA Today, December 13, 2015

Coloring Your World
"The Essentials"

Acknowledgments

Thank you to the following people and organizations
who without their contributions and support this
book could not have been written:

Joe Hardenbrook, whose encouragement, spiritual
guidance provided me the strength to believe in this
project.

Family, Friends and all the many people who
influenced my life.

Jenny @www.fiverr.com/jsholer74, whose
proofreading and editing improved the quality of this
book tremendously.

CreateSpace for making self-publishing possible and
affordable.

Coloring Your World
"The Essentials"

Copyright © 2016 Ian Kirk
All rights reserved.

ISBN: 1530707188
ISBN-13: 978-1530707188

Celtic Mandala Design

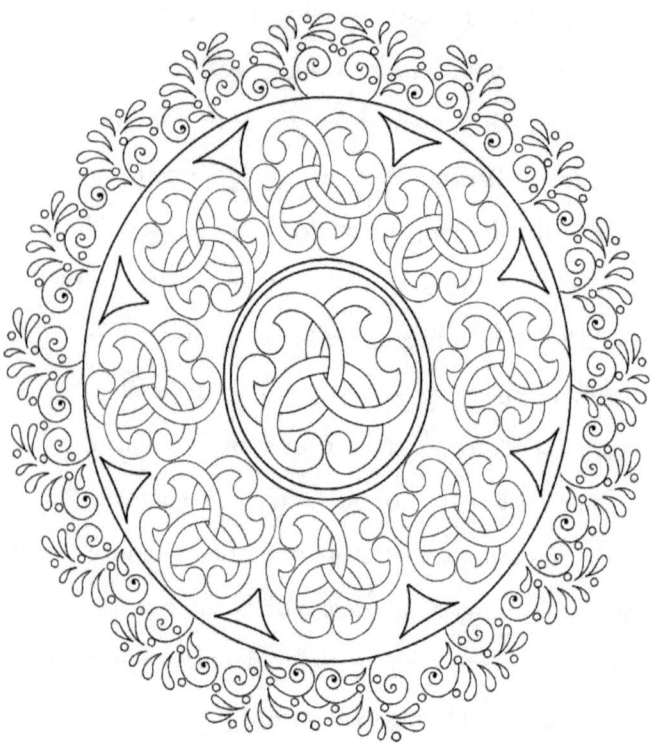

Table of Contents

Contents

INTRODUCTION

Adult coloring books have become a trend recently. It is clear from its very name, "adult coloring book", that it involves colored pencils or crayons and coloring pages. But is it just coloring? How can something like staying within the lines be of benefit to me? I'm sure some of you picked up this book out of curiosity, while others are already aware of the awesome benefits you'll derive from it. I'm happy to tell you that you've made one of the best decisions of this year by buying this book. Let's start with some statistics.

From the English dictionary, the word "coloring" means, "a visual attribute of things that results from the light they emit or transmit or reflect". It is also defined as, "the process or act of changing the color of something". It used to be that the act of coloring was reserved only for children; but recently, the activity has not solely been used by children. Grown-ups now have a lot of fun with these coloring pages too.

A coloring book is a form of book that contains line-art by which the reader uses colored pencils, pens, crayons, and other artistic mediums. Colored pencils and coloring books arose in the United States as a part of the demonstration of the art process. British artist, Joshua Reynolds rendered lectures inspired coloring and drawing field. Previously, coloring had been reserved for children and the adults who occasionally babysat them. This occasional thing, which started as a small hobby, is now an international trend as described before. Today, adult coloring books are available on the greatest best seller lists throughout the world. Adult coloring books have a lot of benefits. This is the reason why they are on shelves, aside from the fun they bring.

Coloring Your World
"The Essentials"

While this book being written (February 2016), top twenty best-selling books involves a quarter of coloring-in books. So now the question arises, what is an adult coloring book? How coloring-in books are currently outselling top fiction authors with many new releases such as Paula Hawkins and E.L. James? Why and how a particular coloring book is different from one another?

Adult coloring book are simply the coloring books for group ups (Adults). They are similar to children coloring books as they are full of different outlined illusions, which are designed to be filled in with colored pencils, crayons, markers, or whatever medium you want to use. We all grew up during the time of doodle art - remember? You got a pack of felt markers and elaborate black-line drawings in a number of themes. We would spend hours coloring them in! Little did we know that coloring pages would have benefits for us. They did back then and still do today, for people of all ages. The themes provided by adult coloring books are usually intricate and centered more on adult images, not your childhood counterparts that included bunnies, superheroes, and farm animals. Now you can expect to see geometric patterns, psychedelic patterns meaningful of doodle art-type pages, fantasy images including angels, dragons, goddesses and mermaids, and ancient designs of a religious and spiritual nature.

Psychedelic

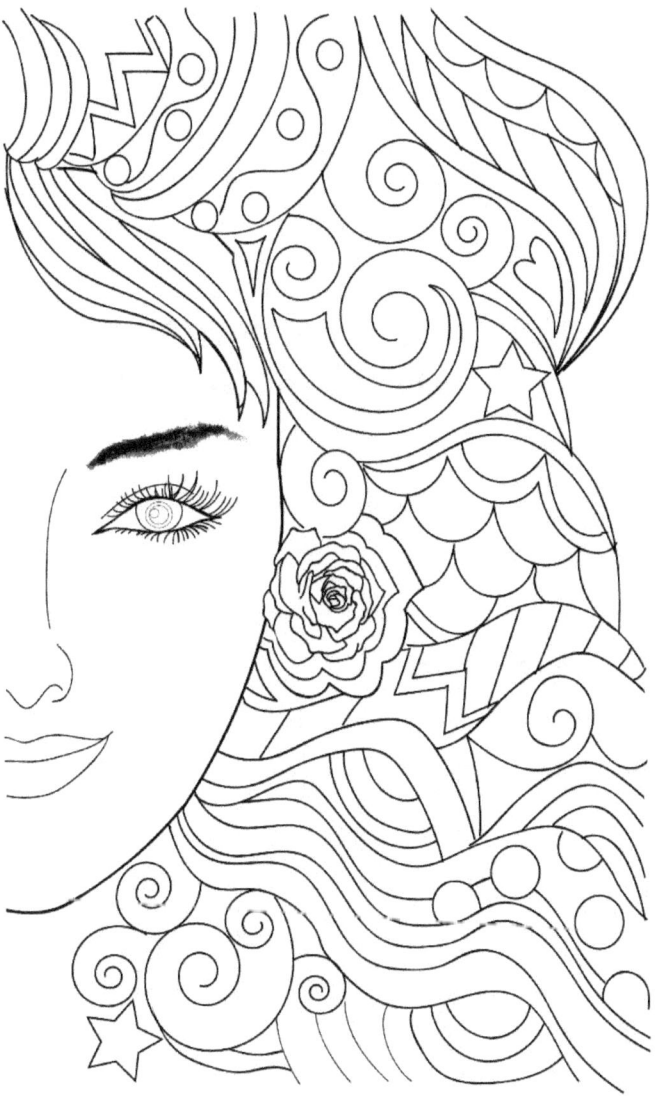

1

ADULT COLORING BOOK ADVANTAGE

Adult coloring books are different from kids' coloring books in the sense that adult books do not contain juvenile designs and images compared to that of kids'. In the arena of television characters, i.e. Barney, superheroes and barnyard animals, adult coloring books are usually filled with:

- Geometric designs
- Natural habitat elements, including flowers, gardens, insects, trees, leaves and animals
- Buildings and cities

Coloring Your World
"The Essentials"

- Anatomical drawings
- Mermaids, angels, and goddesses
- Psychedelic patterns
- Wallpaper patterns
- Celtics designs and mandalas

A coloring book name secret garden was published in 2013 by illustrator, Johanna Basford. The pages of the coloring book showed beautiful hand-illustrated ink drawings. In March of the same year, the New York Times reported about a Korean pop star named Kim Ki Bum, who posted a picture of one of the pages of the Secret Garden on Instagram and at the time, he has around 1.8 million followers on Instagram. The post went viral and started the adult coloring book craze.

The relaxing and stress-relieving features of the book helped feed the book's popularity explosion. Many users' reviews of the book indicated that the low-stress, repetitive nature of coloring was relaxing. Soothing and a method for disconnecting from the stress arising from the pressures of life and work. In the most basic sense, the act of applying a colored medium to intricate line-drawings provides the benefits of relaxation and stress reduction. You are able to put the outside world aside for a moment and focus on the singular act of coloring. Studies have shown that anxiety levels were reduced in adults who colored; however, they did note that simple doodling had no effect on anxiety. The focus on coloring switches off the brain and allows relief from anxiety in that particular moment.

Coloring does not have a need for complicated thought processes and, like listening to calming music, you are able to get within yourself, isolated from external anxiety, commotion and distractions. The repetitive, low-stress and "no brainer" act of coloring lends itself to relaxation. The calming effect not only helps to reduce stress levels, but can also help to bring you back to your youth.

The awesome part is that anyone can do it – with no skill-set required! So, grab a crayon and let's start this amazing coloring journey together by coloring one of the four examples with in this book. You can make it even more enjoyable by having your kids or grandkids color with you.

Zentangle-style

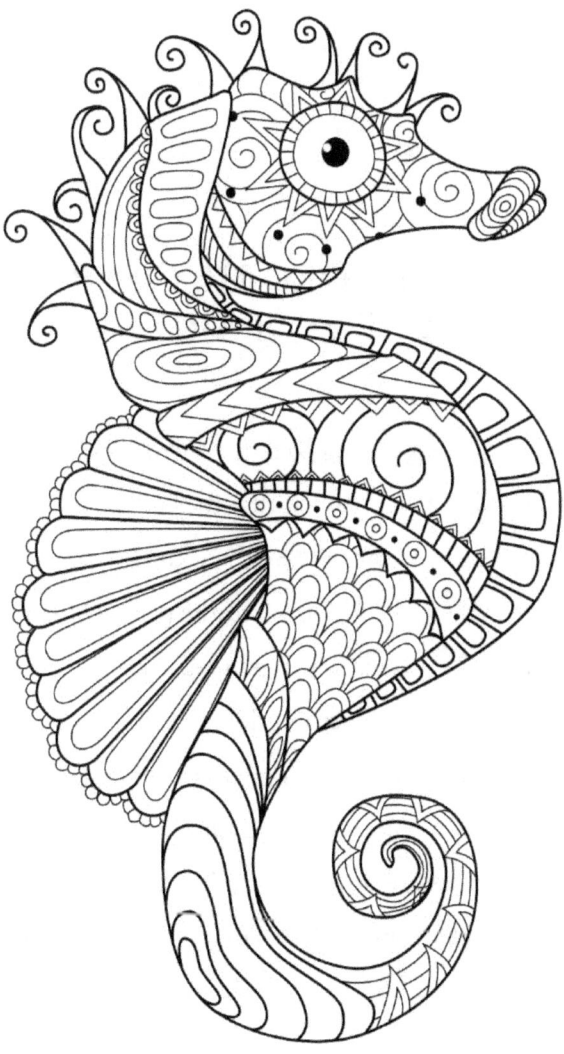

2

WHY ADULT COLORING BOOKS ARE POPULAR?

Adult coloring books bring back the memories of childhood and users explained that they enjoyed reimagining those memories. Adult coloring books have the power to take you back to the past, a much simpler time. They are also providing a way for parents to connect with their children because they can all sit down and draw or color together. For years, parents have been coloring with their children; but now, their choices are no longer limited to children's coloring books like SpongeBob Square Pants or Dora the Explorer.

Coloring Your World
"The Essentials"

Let's take a trip down memory lane. Can you remember when you were a child, lying on the floor on your tummy, your coloring book open, with a colored crayon in-hand and the rest of the crayons scattered out of the box? And then when you started coloring, do you still remember the sense of enjoyment and peace you derived from it? Whenever you see yourself feeling stress or anxiety, you should consider revisiting your favorite childhood memories, like coloring.

Adult coloring books are designed using intricate patterns. These patterns are psychologically-based on alleviating tension. The coloring we find ourselves doing helps us to relax. For this reason, the books have become really popular. The back and forth movement of the colored pencil, marker or crayon has a calming effect on the body and the brain. These actions make use of both sides of the brain, thereby causing neurons to reinforce their connections between both sides and shutting down the frontal lobe that controls organization in the process. This gives a feeling of balance after a stressful day at work. Coloring provides relief to the daily demands of attention given to work, the overload of information, the stress and intensity of everyday life, competition and play.

Natural Habitat Design

3

THE GENERAL HEALING
POWER OF ART

Art is not known to have the ability to cure disease but it can really help an individual to cope with it. Researchers have admitted for years that art has a lot of therapeutic qualities and today, with the help of art therapy, people get to express themselves at times when they find it difficult to speak or when they cannot put their feelings into words because they have been diagnosed with a serious ailment like cancer. In a study which was conducted in 2006 they discovered that art therapy for women suffering from cancer helped them to significantly reduce the symptoms of emotional and physical distress acquired as a result of the course of treatment. In that same year, another study showed adult cancer patients experienced overwhelming comfort and an increased desire to continue with their treatment therapy after just one hour of art therapy.

Very often, people suffering from cancer describe this feeling of their body being overtaken by the cancerous tumor. This is because they are overwhelmed. Coloring books enable them to engage in a creative process. However, it is not just those suffering from cancer that benefit from the visual arts. Adult coloring books are also of great importance to people dealing with other medical conditions, including depression, anxiety, PTSD and dementia.

Art and the act of drawing often involve the use of the art medium as a tool for confronting the specific illness of a patient. In our high school art classes, we observed that some peers were more artistically-gifted than others. This observation is true among patients, as well. Judging yourself a bad artist without trying it first will result in you missing out on great art benefits. Adult coloring allows for creativity and is a

15

means to explore your unknown drawing skills. Your drawing can be used to address your ailments. To do this, you just need to color within the lines and there you are, you will get the desired effect. The lack of zeal for artistic drawings from some patients in an adult coloring program can also be seen as an original form of art therapy.

Adult coloring alone is not art therapy, but it doesn't mean that the activity is not a helpful aspect of art therapy. An art therapy student of Lesley University, Citerella, reported to Medical Daily that in her experience, she has seen many adults using the coloring books both in therapy and in classes to help them to focus. She reported that a large number of her graduate classmates brought the coloring books to class and used them as a tool to redirect their focus onto the lectures being presented. Many professors are starting to accept this behavior. She explained that during her internship, she found that fidgeting clients occasionally asked for coloring books to allow them to fully concentrate during group discussions. The inability to focus is oftentimes a symptom of stress or anxiety, so it makes a lot of sense that adult coloring books will help to relieve those feelings. Coloring is similar to meditation in the sense that while coloring, you enter into a relaxing mindset similar to what you achieve through meditation. Coloring helps take away the brain's attention from other thoughts and focus only on the moment-at-hand. Coloring, as well as knitting, is calming and has a physical effect on our body. With the assistance of coloring, the most amazing things happen. Particularly in patients, changes were observed in brain waves and heart rate when coloring. These changes resulted from the attention given to the patterns and details while coloring.

Dr. Joel Pearson, a brain scientist from the University of New South Wales, explained the therapeutic effect of coloring in a different way. He said that fully-concentrating on coloring an image aids in the replacement of negative images and thoughts with positive ones. Your brain tells you to pick a color, look at edges, size and shape. These thoughts occupy the parts of the brain that stop anxiety-related imagery.

Coloring Your World
"The Essentials"

One of the best forms of meditation is coloring. When we were little, we had this fresh innocence and, at the time, we were not burdened with responsibility and expectations from spouses, parents, and employers. So when we color, our brain takes us back to that childhood time. Picking up a crayon now will help us to revisit our childhood past, which was filled with a sense of simplicity. Coloring allows you to experience a little fun and allows your inner child to come out. Coloring helps to quiet your mind, thereby slowing down.

Geometric Design

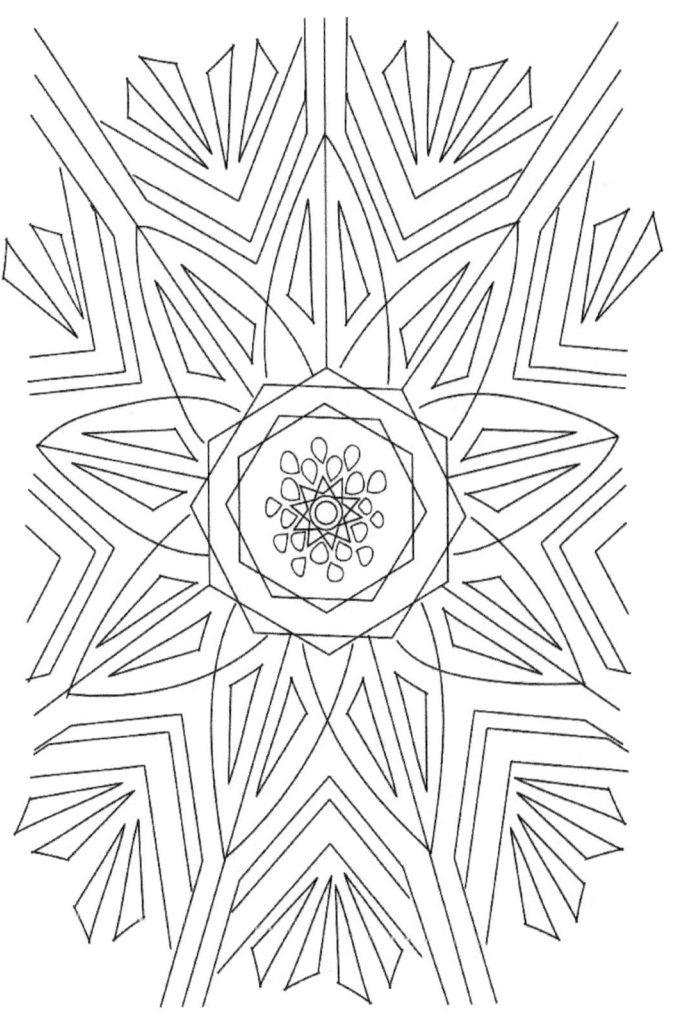

4

WHAT HAPPENS WHEN WE COLOR?

As an adult, you have privilege to color your pictures outside the borders of an illustrations. You can keep your colorings sophisticated or you can also keep it simple. For an affordable fee, you can get a coloring book and box of crayons. Nothing is as good as the soothing smell of new crayons and a fresh coloring book. You can also search different sites online that offer free and printer-friendly coloring pages. On a related note, you may feel like you have outgrown crayons and instead, want to color using a medium with a different texture and feel. An affordable alternative is a felt pen and pencil crayons. You can also spend a little more money and get oil pastels, colored pencils, watercolor pencils and Conte crayons. Today, coloring books are widely-used for marketing and promoting TV cartoon characters and children's movies.

I'm sure after all you've read about adult coloring, you are now ready to take action to enjoy its numerous benefits. I'm happy to tell you that I've tried it and it's amazing. I'm sure you'll have a sweet story to tell too, once you start coloring for yourself. All the best!!!

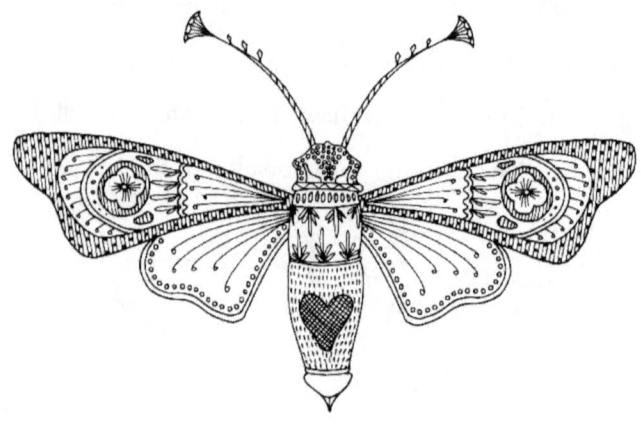

ABOUT THE AUTHOR

Ian Kirk is an entrepreneur and author who loves to help and serve others. Coloring Your World is his first published book. It was written because of his own experiences with health, stress and anxiety. Ian discovered great relief from his stress and anxiety when he took up drawing as a hobby. He hopes to help others who are likewise living heath issues or are stress out. May you experience peace in your life always.